ideals CHRISTMAS

65TH ANNIVERSARY EDITION

A special anniversary collection of
classic selections from the past
and new favorites

*As the name implies, these are books of clean, wholesome,
old-fashioned American ideals—homey philosophy,
poetry, art, music, neighborliness—things many of us
may overlook during our busy days.*

—DESCRIPTION FROM EARLY EDITIONS OF *IDEALS* MAGAZINE

IDEALS PUBLICATIONS

NASHVILLE, TENNESSEE

December

Craig E. Sathoff

The coziness around the hearth,
Each brightly glowing ember,
Brings peace and warmth and
    harbor from
The cold winds of December.

December likes to roar and hiss
And cloak the earth with snow
And then just settle back and watch
The snowmen as they grow.

It is a time for merriment
And hitching up the sleigh

To gallop through the brittle air
In spirits light and gay.

Hot chocolate and caroling
And gifts we must remember,
The message of our dear
    Christ's birth
Are all parts of December.

It is a sparkling, tinseled month
That's full of joy and cheer;
It gives a luster that remains
Throughout the coming year.

From CHRISTMAS IDEALS 1992

Photograph by Maura McEvoy/Botanica/Jupiter Images

This Night Called Christmas

Eileen Spinelli

Though storm may follow,
frost spark later air—
though other nights fall faded,
frayed with care—
this night
of candles
casting tasseled light,
of children's snowy carols,
voices bright,
of friends on doorsteps,
sounds of bells above—
this night called Christmas
tethers us to love.

Though worry spoons
a gloomy wait-and-see,
this night we dance
around the tinseled tree.
We giggle underneath
the mistletoe

and gladden every present
with a bow.
We tie a sprig of holly
to each toy.
This night called Christmas
tethers us to joy.

Though anger lingers
in a darkened place,
this night is sweet
with welcome and with grace.
And no one need be lonely
or apart.

An angel's tidings
comforts every heart
and beckons us to where
all quarrels cease.
This night called Christmas
tethers us to peace.

Painting by Jay Killian. Image from Ideals Publications

Letter from Home

Gladys Taber

Now the fire of another year is burning low as December blows a dusting of snow over the hills, over the valleys. There is a lovely feeling when the world turns white. But there is a sadness when the last page of the calendar appears. This is the natural condition of man, I think—to be reluctant to let go of the known and face toward the unknown.

As I let the cockers in and wait while the Irish makes up her mind to stop chasing things, I wonder if this is the beginning of another cold winter. Indoors, Erma already has the house shining. Soon she will bring in greens and decorate for Christmas. I always make a start, but branches have a way of falling down on me. For Erma they hang gracefully where they should. And she climbs up and garlands the outside lamppost so that when the children drive down the road, Christmas comes to meet them.

When the first heavy snow comes, around Christmas, the house begins to smell of damp mittens, melting snow, rubbers, and wet fur. It is a good homey smell. And it blends with the spicy odor of pine, the aroma of oyster stew, and the smell of sage and basted turkey. At holidaytime, breakfast at Stillmeadow becomes important. We have hot cakes with golden maple syrup and tiny crisp sausages. Eggs baked in cream. Creamed finnan haddie. (This was Jill's favorite, and now her son fixes it for us.)

In my childhood New England, breakfasts were robust, to say the least. At Uncle Walter's we had baked beans and codfish cakes Sunday morning. There were two bean pots, one with unsweetened beans for Uncle Walter, one rich with molasses and crusty with salt pork for the rest of us. At Grandfather's we might have pork chops, creamy potatoes, and warm slices of apple pie. Or fresh-caught fish, fried golden brown.

Grandmother would have been horrified at today's menus, for she liked to set a good table. There might be ten or more at the huge row table, but there was always more than enough. If a neighbor dropped in to see Grandfather, a chair was pulled up, and he helped himself to apple fritters, peppery country sausage cakes, light rolls, and, of course, pie. The coffeepot was never empty. The big enamel pot stayed on the back of the range all day, and the coffee must have been terrible; but I had mine with half milk and thought it was delicious.

A special quality of December is that it brings us close to the daily lives of others who are dear to us but far away. As Christmas cards and notes come in, I feel that I am back in time with old friends. I am glad to know that Charlotte has another grandchild, but I see her as a girl with windy hair and laughter like golden bells. I am

Historic Captain E. Harding Home, Chatham, Cape Cod, Massachusetts. Photograph by William H. Johnson

back in the parlor (for we had parlors in my small town), and she is playing "Maple Leaf Rag" (by ear), because that is what I always asked for.

The days grow shorter now, and this I do not like. I am addicted to long dreamy twilights. In the country, however, we live by the light, so we have supper early. By midafternoon the chores are done, and the fire on the hearth is burning sweet with apple.

Christmas Eve is the time for carols and for sitting around the fire and talking about the past and future. The tree glows in the light of the candles on the trestle table. When the house quiets down, I sit a few moments watching the firelight and thinking what a fortunate house Stillmeadow is to have small feet pattering around on the wide oak floorboards. I wonder how many youngsters have taken their first steps in this room since 1690.

When I poke the embers back and go to the front door and step out a minute to say good night to the world, the cockers and Holly, the Irish, go with me. There are others, too, whose presence I feel. Jill, my beloved companion of years, stands in the doorway as she's always stood, tall and quiet. Honey, the golden cocker who spent fourteen years with us, drifts across the snow, her silken ears starred with flakes. All those I have loved are not lost. I share with them my good night to friends known and unknown.

From CHRISTMAS IDEALS *1973*

Christmas in the Home

Judith Lane

Christmas is a very special time of the year for friends and relatives and hearth-warmed reunions. Home becomes the focal point during this intimate celebration. Home is a traditionally trimmed, gift-wrapped place.

As the nights lengthen and the wintry winds arrive and the outdoors turns crispy-cold, the inside radiates warmth from a blazing fire. The kitchen fills with sugary smells, and the rooms are illuminated by multicolored lights of merriment.

A beautifully grown, freshly cut evergreen stands majestically. The aroma of the forest saturates the home; the perfume of pine permeates the farthest corner. Upon the top of this Christmas tree, a star is placed.

The branches of the tree open wide to welcome its ornaments: a little blue bird from Aunt Martha, a ragged cloth candy cane made by a child some years ago, brightly colored balls—new—replacing the ones the cat had friskily pawed, and the shimmering icicles placed with deliberate care.

The manger is dusted, the sweet faces of Christmas are tenderly wiped of their summer slumber, and under this most beautiful of trees, the story of Christmas is arranged—like last year, like next year.

Out come the Christmas stockings, of deepest red trimmed with slightly yellowed white cuffs of a childhood. Anxiously the stockings are hung with nails carefully placed in last year's holes. The little green elf appears in the most unlikely place, hopping about, the jester of the season.

Dishes filled with candy tidbits, nuts, and fruit and plates of patterned cookies abound to tempt the appetite. Packages spirited from underneath beds, from on top of closet shelves, from inside dresser drawers tempt the imagination. A plump turkey wrapped in brown paper in the freezer awaits the cranberries and the chestnut dressing.

On the front door of the home, a wreath laced with snowflakes and a large red ribbon gives a clue to what awaits inside. The porch light casts a soft glow upon the newly fallen snow; a bell rings inside the house.

Home, traditionally trimmed for this Christmas season, opens its door and welcomes the traveler. Christmas is the season for visiting and sharing and remembering. The remembrance of home remains throughout the year to be refurbished again another season.

From CHRISTMAS IDEALS *1982*

Photograph by Jessie Walker

Old-Fashioned Cards
Ogden Nash

Oh, give me an old-fashioned Christmas card
With hostlers hostling in an old inn yard,
With church bells chiming their silver notes,
And jolly red squires in their jolly red coats,
And a good fat goose by the fire that dangles,
And a few more angels and a few less angles.
Turn backward, Time, to please this bard,
And give me an old-fashioned Christmas card.

Christmas Cards
Edna Jacques

How lovely are the sentiments
Contained in Christmas cards,
As well as dear heartwarming scenes
Of snowy trees and yards.

They never change so very much,
But who would want it so?
For Christmas seems to just belong
To cedar trees and snow.

The greetings on a Christmas card
Are precious as a gem
Because old neighbors and old friends
Send us their love with them . . .

Warming our hearts with loving words,
Making us know that they
Are thinking of dear bygone times
Upon this Christmas Day.

A holly wreath, a little church,
A lovely lighted door,
Some carol singers in the street,
The windows of a store—

All these are part of Christmastime,
Like cake and mistletoe,
Because a card arrived today
And sort of told me so.

From CHRISTMAS IDEALS *1973*

Photograph by Jessie Walker

Christmas Trees

(A Christmas Circular Letter)

Robert Frost

The city had withdrawn into itself
And left at last the country to the country;
When between whirls of snow not come to lie
And whirls of foliage not yet laid, there drove
A stranger to our yard, who looked the city,
Yet did in country fashion in that there
He sat and waited till he drew us out
A-buttoning coats to ask him who he was.
He proved to be the city come again
To look for something it had left behind
And could not do without and keep its
    Christmas.
He asked if I would sell my Christmas trees;
My woods—the young fir balsams like a place
Where houses all are churches and have spires.
I hadn't thought of them as Christmas trees.
I doubt if I was tempted for a moment
To sell them off their feet to go in cars
And leave the slope behind the house all bare,
Where the sun shines now no warmer than
    the moon.
I'd hate to have them know it if I was.
Yet more I'd hate to hold my trees except
As others hold theirs or refuse for them,
Beyond the time of profitable growth,
The trial by market everything must come to.
I dallied so much with the thought of selling.
Then whether from mistaken courtesy
And fear of seeming short of speech, or whether
From hope of hearing good of what was mine,
I said, "There aren't enough to be worthwhile."
"I could soon tell how many they would cut,
You let me look them over."

"You could look.
But don't expect I'm going to let you have them."
Pasture they spring in, some in clumps too close
That lop each other of boughs, but not a few
Quite solitary and having equal boughs
All round and round. The latter he nodded
    "Yes" to,
Or paused to say beneath some lovelier one,
With a buyer's moderation, "That would do."
I thought so too, but wasn't there to say so.
We climbed the pasture on the south, crossed over,
And came down on the north.
He said, "A thousand."

"A thousand Christmas trees!—at what apiece?"

He felt some need of softening that to me:
"A thousand trees would come to thirty dollars."

Then I was certain I had never meant
To let him have them. Never show surprise!
But thirty dollars seemed so small beside
The extent of pasture I should strip, three cents
(For that was all they figured out apiece),
Three cents so small beside the dollar friends
I should be writing to within the hour
Would pay in cities for good trees like those,
Regular vestry trees whole Sunday Schools
Could hang enough on to pick off enough.
A thousand Christmas trees I didn't know I had!
Worth three cents more to give away than sell
As may be shown by a simple calculation.
Too bad I couldn't lay one in a letter.
I can't help wishing I could send you one
In wishing you herewith a Merry Christmas.

Rachel's Little Star Tree

Elisabeth Weaver Winstead

Five-year-old Josh, my nephew, was speechless with excitement. He was to spend the weekend with us in the country, and he had been promised his very own Christmas tree. From our woods, he was to select a choice evergreen to take home to his parents and two-year-old sister, Rachel.

We trudged with a happy, observant little boy across the icy fields to the nearby woods. Not feeling the cold, Josh ran ahead, singing "Jingle Bells" with all his heart.

Our choices were abundant. We examined pine trees and cedar trees, tall trees and short trees, large trees and small trees. But at each one, Josh merely shook his head. After pointing out more than twenty evergreens, we had not found a single tree that he liked. We continued looking and urged Josh to choose one, but to no avail. None was good enough.

Now it was beginning to snow; and a cold, stinging wind whistled through the trees. It was time to make a choice and go home.

Finally, Josh pointed to a cedar tree that was barely five feet tall. "That's my tree," he stated.

We were puzzled by his selection; there were so many larger and more handsome trees around us. "Wouldn't you like a bigger one?" my husband asked.

"No, I'm sure this is just right," he replied firmly. "It's just right for Rachel."

"But this is your tree, not Rachel's," we reminded him.

"I have to keep my promise," he replied solemnly.

"What promise?" we both asked, surprised.

"You see," explained Josh, "I promised Rachel I'd find a tree that was just her size so she could stand in her high chair and put the star on top all by herself. That's what I promised her at home. That was our secret."

Watching the delighted child beside his tree, we felt his joy and warmth at unselfishly remembering another—the real spirit of the season. We shared his excitement as the small evergreen crackled with each stroke of the axe and then fell.

Homeward bound at last, we sang a resounding last chorus of "Jingle Bells" as the sky darkened and we left the woods behind. We would always remember how a thoughtful five-year-old boy had reminded us of the real meaning of Christmas; and the tiny green tree we dragged behind us would always be remembered as "Rachel's Little Star Tree."

From CHRISTMAS IDEALS *1987*

Tell Me a Story of Christmas

Bill Vaughan

"Tell me a story of Christmas," she said. The television mumbled faint inanities in the next room. From a few houses down the block came the sounds of car doors and of guests being greeted.

Her father thought awhile. His mind went back over the interminable parade of Christmas books he had read at the bedside of his children.

"Well," he started tentatively, "once upon a time, it was the week before Christmas, all little elves at the North Pole were sad. . . ."

"I'm tired of elves," she whispered. And he could tell she was tired, maybe almost as weary as he was himself after the last few feverish days.

"Okay," he said. "There was once, in a city not far from here, the cutest wriggly little puppy you ever saw. The snow was falling, and this little puppy didn't have a home. As he walked along the streets, he saw a house that looked quite a bit like our house. And at the window—"

"Was a little girl who looked quite a bit like me," she said with a sigh. "I'm tired of puppies. I love Pinky, of course. I mean story puppies."

"Okay," he said. "No puppies. This narrows the field."

"What?"

"Nothing. I'll think of something. Oh, sure. There was a forest, way up in the north, farther even than where Uncle Ed lives. And all the trees were talking about how each one was going to be the grandest Christmas tree of all. One said, 'I'm going to be a Christmas tree too.' And all the trees laughed and laughed and said: 'A Christmas tree? You? Who would want you?'"

"No trees, Daddy," she said. "We have a tree at school and at Sunday school and at the supermarket and downstairs and a little one in my room. I am very tried of trees."

"You are very spoiled," he said.

"Hmmm," she replied. "Tell me a Christmas story."

"Let's see. All the reindeer up at the North Pole were looking forward to pulling Santa's sleigh. All but one, and he felt sad because—" He began with a jolly ring in his voice but quickly realized that this wasn't going to work either. His daughter didn't say anything; she just looked at him reproachfully.

"Tired of reindeer too?" he asked. "Frankly, so am I. How about Christmas on the farm when I was a little boy? Would you like to hear about how it was in the olden days, when my grandfather would heat up bricks and put them in the sleigh and we'd all go for a ride?"

"Yes, Daddy," she said obediently. "But not right now. Not tonight."

He was silent, thinking. His repertoire was exhausted. She was quiet too. Maybe, he thought, I'm home free. Maybe she has gone to sleep.

"Daddy," she murmured. "Tell me a story of Christmas."

Then it was as though he could read the words, so firmly were they in his memory. Still holding her hand, he leaned back:

"And it came to pass in those days, that there went out a decree from Caesar Augustus, that all the world should be taxed . . ."

Her hand tightened a bit in his, and he told her a story of Christmas.

Such Simple Things
Deborah A. Bennett

The cardboard star
of silver glitter,
the clothespin deer
with button nose,
the crocheted snowman
beginning to wither,
the macaroni angel
with ribbons and bows.

The tinfoil lamb,
the walnut manger,
the colored paper garland
round the tree.
The children abed
and we by the fire,
dream how lovely such
simple things can be.

When clustered sparks
Of many-colored fire
Appear at night
In ordinary windows,

We hear and sing
The customary carols.

They bring us ragged miracles
And hay and candles
And flowering weeds of poetry
That are loved all the more
Because they are so common.

—Anne Porter

Photograph by Jessie Walker

The Christmas Cat
Marcia K. Leaser

On padded feet the little cat
came silently creeping by.
Dad swears he never saw him—
neither did Sis, my mom, nor I.
But nonetheless, the whiskered pest
sneaked past four sets of eyes.

When next viewed, our furry friend
was grinning and purring with glee.
I looked at Dad, my sis, and Mom,
and they three looked at me.
Then we all laughed,
     for the sly little cat
was atop the Christmas tree.

Do Not Open Until Christmas
James S. Tippett

I shake-shake,
Shake-shake,
Shake the package well.
But what there is
Inside of it,
Shaking will not tell.

Bundles
John Farrar

A bundle is a funny thing;
It always sets me wondering.
For whether it is thin or wide
You never know just what's inside.

Especially on Christmas week,
Temptation is so great to peek!
Now wouldn't it be much more fun
If shoppers carried things undone?

Christmas Morning

Jeanne Conte

I try hard to sleep, knowing that the sooner I fall asleep, the quicker the morning comes. I envision the pretty scene downstairs: The tree stands tall, all the way to the ceiling. It is wide-spreading and decorated with tinsel and bright-colored balls. Silver icicles hang all over the tree, falling long and reflecting the colors of the tree lights. Cotton snow surrounds its base, barely covering the white sheet peeking out here and there as if wishing to join the festivities.

And there, under the tall tree, under its glittering branches, rests the subject of the celebration—the tiny baby Jesus with arms outstretched, too, as if welcoming and condoning this warm ritual of the observance of His birthday. Around Him are the presents, just small human semblances in memory of the greatest gift—Jesus. The gifts are wrapped in various colorful designs or in red or white tissue paper with bowed ribbons.

I am still awake. It is Christmas Eve, and everybody around me is now fast asleep. Finally my body begins to give in, but it must be near dawn. No one is to go downstairs before six A.M., and no one is to wake up anybody else. I finally fall asleep, and instantly there is a ruckus! The boys are whooping, the girls are stretching and grabbing their bathrobes, and Mother is calling up the stairs: "Good *morniiing. It's Chriiistmas!*"

We tumble downstairs. As some of us line up for the bathroom, others group into the grandparents' dressing closet or bedroom, jerking arms through sweaters and legs through long stockings. We quickly appear in our finest clothes.

The rule is well-known. No one enters the Christmas tree area—the living room—until the grandparents say so. And that is after we're dressed and all have finished breakfast in Grandmother's kitchen, where tables are set in long rows of boards laid across sawhorses and topped with clean, white tablecloths, nicely set.

We are finally assembled, and Grandfather reads from the Bible the story of the birth of Jesus. He asks the blessing and we begin. Our spoons dive into hot oatmeal, and it takes so long to finish, even with warm, melted brown sugar oozing all around the milk in our bowls. We have to wait politely until everyone is through, sitting and fidgeting with smiles cracking our faces until we are finally ready.

We tear into the big room to find the socks we gave Grandmother—the largest each of us had—and they aren't hanging up anymore, but heavy with fruit, candy, nuts, and a few secrets stuffed within. They lay in a row on the floor with other gifts alongside—treasures guessed and unguessed, asked for and unasked for.

We gather our socks and their contents and sit around the big room on the floor by our par-

Photograph by Dianne Dietrich Leis/Dietrich Photography

ents. Everyone sits quietly, waiting for Grandmother to appoint one of us to distribute the gifts. We open them one by one, not in a frenzy like with the socks. Grandmother's gift to me is crocheted dresses for my Shirley Temple doll, and they fit into the doll trunk. I watch, staring closely at faces as the gifts I brought are opened. I worry lest they aren't liked, but they are liked. I can tell.

Then we're hurried into coats and scarves (many of them new), and I stuff my hands into my new white bunny-fur muff. We head off to the church—the strange, different church of our grandparents. The music swells, rising and lowering and surrounding us with the most joyful sounds I've ever heard. I sit enthralled and entranced and hear again the story of how God gave us the baby Jesus.

Then it's back to my grandparents' warm house, where we cousins play and talk while our mothers stir around the kitchen. Wonderful smells waft through the house, melding with happy talk and the sounds of children playing new games and examining new toys. One cousin got a tape recorder, and he hides it here and there, guffawing when we catch him at it.

An aunt sits at the piano, and Christmas hymns begin to float through the room. After a time of enjoyment and leisure, we girls are called to help Grandmother by setting the table or chopping carrots for the salad or stuffing cheese into celery. We quickly carry heaping bowls full of tasty hot food into the dining room.

The big table is long and beautiful and soon heavy with food. We children have our own tables with the sawhorses underneath, and we sidle around, saving places for favorite cousins. Everyone comes to dinner and Grandfather says grace again. Each of us delights in this fine dinner, and all is warmth and happiness. We are filled with wonder, still, of the story of the birth of the Child of God sent down to us from heaven, and the spirit of it enfolds us in its amazing warmth.

What Is Christmas?

Alice Leedy Mason

What is Christmas?

Can you guess?
Time to spread some happiness,
Children trying extra hard,
Folks remembered with a card,
Hearth fires burning warm and red,
Bright star shining overhead,
Preparations being made,
Special music softly played.

What is Christmas?

Come and see
Decorations on the tree,
Homemade cookies, candy canes,
Lovely stained-glass windowpanes.
See the wreath upon the door;
Sacred signs appear once more—
Life-size créche or tiny scene,
Lighted tapers, tall and lean.

What is Christmas?

Gifts to share,
Touch of winter on the air,
Carols sung and Christmas plays,
Celebrating many ways,
Trimming trees with ball and twine,
Pungent fragrance of the pine,
Holly, mistletoe and bell—
All these add their magic spell.

What is Christmas?

Peace and joy,
Memories for each girl and boy
Strengthen family ties once more,
Greet the stranger at the door.
Prayer and praise are lifted high
Over church spires to the sky.
Christmas shared is never gone;
Love itself will linger on.

From CHRISTMAS IDEALS *1981*

Guessing Time

Edgar A. Guest

It's guessing time at our house;
Every evening after tea
We start guessing what old
    Santa's going
To leave us on our tree.
Every one of us holds secrets
That the others try to steal
And that eyes and lips are
    plainly having
Trouble to conceal.
And a little lip that quivered just
A bit the other night
Was a sad and startling warning that
I mustn't guess it right.

"Guess what you'll get for Christmas!"
Is the cry that starts the fun.
And I answer: "Give the letter
With which the name's begun."
Oh, the eyes that dance around me
And the joyous faces there
Keep me nightly guessing wildly:
"Is it something I can wear?"
I implore them all to tell me
In a frantic sort of way
And pretend that I am puzzled,
Just to keep them feeling gay.

Oh, the wise and knowing glances
That across the table fly
And the winks, exchanged
    with Mother,
That they think I never spy;
Oh, the whispered confidences
That are poured into her ear,
And the laughter gay that follows
When I try my best to hear!
Oh, the shouts of glad
    derision when
I bet that it's a cane,
And the merry answering chorus:
"No it's not. Just guess again!"

It's guessing time at our house,
And the fun is running fast,
And I wish somehow this contest
Of delight could always last.
For the love that's in their faces
And their laughter ringing clear
Is their dad's most precious present
When the Christmastime is near.
And soon as it is over,
When the tree is bare and plain,
I shall start in looking forward
To the time to guess again.

A CHRISTMAS MORNING *by Lee Stroneck. Artwork courtesy of the artist and Wild Wings*

Keeping Christmas

Henry van Dyke

It is a good thing to observe Christmas Day. The mere marking of times and seasons, when men agree to stop work and make merry together, is a wise and wholesome custom. It helps one to feel the supremacy of the common life over the individual life. It reminds a man to set his own little watch, now and then, by the great clock of humanity which runs on sun time.

But there is a better thing than the observance of Christmas Day, and that is keeping Christmas.

Are you willing to forget what you have done for other people and to remember what other people have done for you; to ignore what the world owes you and to think what you owe the world; to put your rights in the background and your duties in the middle distance and your chances to do a little more than your duty in the foreground; to see that your fellow men are just as real as you are and try to look behind their faces to their hearts, hungry for joy; to own that probably the only good reason for your existence is not what you are going to get out of life but what you are going to give to life; to close your book of complaints against the management of the universe and look around you for a place where you can sow a few seeds of happiness—are you willing to do these things for even a day? Then you can keep Christmas.

Are you willing to stoop down and reconsider the needs and desires of little children; to remember the weakness and loneliness of people who are growing old; to stop asking how much your friends love you, and ask yourself whether you love them enough; to bear in mind the things that other people have to bear on their hearts; to try to understand what those who live in the same house with you really want, without waiting for them to tell you; to trim your lamp so that it will give more light and less smoke; and to carry it in front so that your shadow will fall behind you; to make a grave for your ugly thoughts and a garden for your kind feelings with the gate open— are you willing to do these things even for a day? Then you can keep Christmas.

Are you willing to believe that love is the strongest thing in the world— stronger than hate, stronger than death— and that the blessed life which began in Bethlehem nineteen hundred years ago is the image and brightness of Eternal Love? Then you can keep Christmas.

And if you keep it for a day, why not always? But you can never keep it alone.

From CHRISTMAS IDEALS *1944*

Softly the Night Is Sleeping

Author Unknown

Softly the night is sleeping on Bethlehem's peaceful hill,
Silent the shepherds watching; their gentle flocks are still.
But hark! The wondrous music falls from the opening sky;
Valley and cliff re-echo glory to God on high.
Glory to God it rings again,
Peace on earth, goodwill to men.

Come with the gladsome shepherds, quick hastening
    from the fold,
Come with the wise men bringing incense and
    myrrh and gold,
Come to Him poor and lowly, around the cradle throng,
Come with your hearts of sunshine and sing the
    angel's song.
Glory to God tell out again,
Peace on earth, goodwill to men.

Weave ye the wreath unfading, the fir tree and the pine,
Green from the snows of winter to deck the holy shrine;
Bring ye the happy children, for this is Christmas morn;
Jesus the sinless infant, Jesus the Lord is born.
Glory to God, to God again,
Peace on earth, goodwill to men.

Sing a Song of Christmas
Gail Brook Burket

Sing a song of Christmas—
Of starlight on the snow,
Of scarlet flames of Yuletide logs
And candles' golden glow.
Sing a song of Christmas—
Of mistletoe and pine,
Of holly wreaths and balsam trees
Whose lights and tinsel shine.

Sing a song of Christmas—
Of bells which gaily ring,
And carols on the frosty air
The strolling minstrels sing.
Sing a song of Christmas—
Of happiness and cheer,
And love which lights the earth with joy
To bless the coming year.

From CHRISTMAS IDEALS *1964*

Hello, Again
Nina Gertrude Smith

Hello, again, it's Christmas! in the postman's ring,
In a little child's face, on the snowbird's wing;

In the "*sh-sh-sh*" of secrets; colors, sounds, and smells—
In a stranger's warm, sweet laughter hear the golden bells!

Christmas in the sacred story of a Yuletide's song,
In a new re-captured glory righting every wrong.

In the joy of giving, giving . . . Christmas in the air;
Faith and hope and love are living—
Christmas, Christmas, everywhere!

From CHRISTMAS IDEALS *1951*

This painting by George Hinke appeared in CHRISTMAS IDEALS *1946. Image from Ideals Publications*

Pages from the Past
OF Ideals
MAGAZINE
~∞o@o∞~

Ideals magazine was begun in 1944 with a Christmas issue printed by Van B. Hooper, a public relations manager for a Milwaukee, Wisconsin, manufacturer. The magazine, which had started as bits and pieces of poetry and homey philosophy added to his company's newsletter, struck a chord in its readers. Circulation grew through word of mouth, and at the magazine's height, eight issues a year were published with various themes. The Christmas issue has always been the most popular and has been a Christmastime tradition in countless homes for decades. Although the magazine has since been relocated to Nashville, Tennessee, and many years have passed, the values demonstrated in its pages are unchanged and continue to inspire readers. Today, *Ideals* is still treasured by families who believe that no matter how times change, the vital things—family ties, love of country, and faith in God—are what see us through.

Below are selected covers from throughout the history of IDEALS *magazine. The following six pages are displayed as they appeared in earlier issues. As this special section illustrates, times have changed. But what have not changed, and what* IDEALS *has celebrated for sixty-five years, are the timeless values and pure joys of Christmas.*

Clockwise, from top left: CHRISTMAS IDEALS *1944,* CHRISTMAS IDEALS *1948,* CHRISTMAS IDEALS *1951,*
CHRISTMAS IDEALS *1961,* CHRISTMAS IDEALS *1977,* CHRISTMAS IDEALS *1983,* CHRISTMAS IDEALS *1986,* CHRISTMAS IDEALS *1995*

Let Us Go Back!

Frank H. Keith

Let us go back to the beauties
That are pocketed deep in our past,
The joys we relinquished with childhood
But which hauntingly linger and last!

Let us return to the Christmas
That remains with the children of time—
The Christmas of wonderful wishes,
Of stardust, and snowdrift, and chime!

Let us go back to the vision
Of evergreen peace in our rooms,
Gay ribbons on gifts of the giving,
And the dream that consistenly blooms.

Let us in piety wander
Where the veil of the centuries parts
To look at a crib and an infant,
And Christmas will live in our hearts!

Hang Up the Baby's Stocking

Author Unknown

Hang up the baby's stocking;
Be sure you don't forget
The dear little dimpled darling
Has never seen Christmas yet;
But I've told her all about it,
And she opened her big blue eyes,
And I'm sure she understands it . . .
She looked so funny and wise.

*Dear, what a tiny stocking!
It doesn't take much to hold
Such little pink toes as baby's
Away from the frost and cold.
But then, for the baby's Christmas,
It will never do at all;
For Santa wouldn't be looking
For anything half so small.*

I know what I'll do for the baby;
I've thought of the very best plan . . .
I'll borrow a stocking from Grandma,
The longest that ever I can;
And you'll hang it by mine, dear Mother,
Right here in the corner, so!
And write a letter to Santa.
And fasten it on the toe.

*Write,"This is the baby's stocking
That hangs in the corner here;
You never have seen her, Santa,
For she only came this year;
But she's just the blessedest baby,
And now, before you go,
Just cram her stocking with goodies
From the top clear down to the toe."*

Christmas Morning

Gail O. Clark

The poignant scent of oranges and pine,
The glow of the lights as they gleam and shine,
The crisp crinkly papers of red and of green,
Childish anticipation, all this sets the scene;
That most magical hour of the slow-moving year
At last has arrived . . . Christmas morning is here!

The children fly down, hardly touching the stair.
They descend on the gifts and treasures there.
Such sounds of hasty tearing and ripping,
The packages fly, look, the tree is near tipping!
Soon calm is restored with smiles and good cheer,
And on the children's faces, the message . . .
Christmas morning is here!

©

Pages from the Past 1971

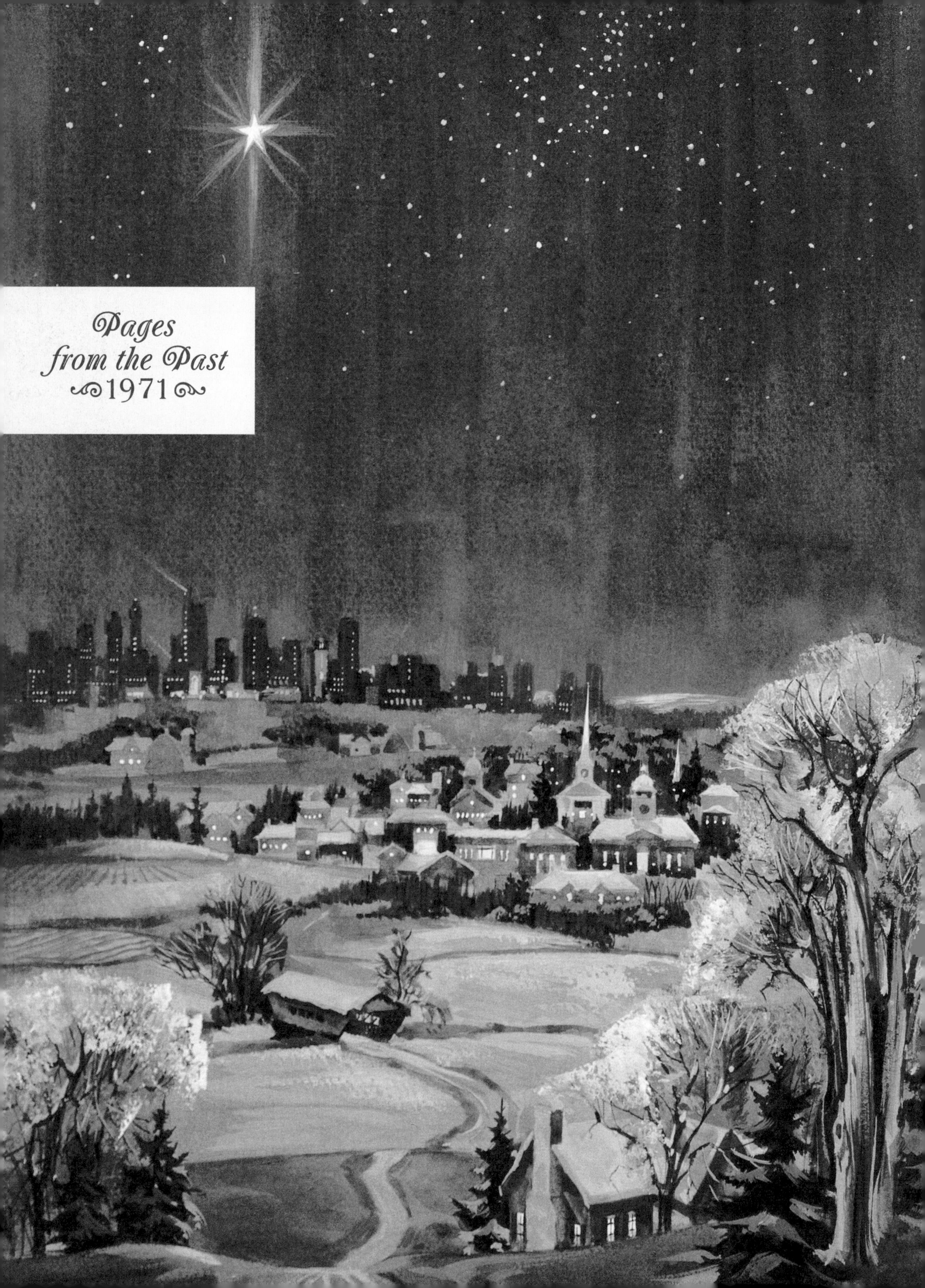

Where Is the Star?

Naomi I. Parks

Where is the Star of Bethlehem
That shone so long ago,
And kept its silent vigil
O'er the stable there below?
Did it vanish forevermore
At the closing of that night,
Or have our hearts been hardened
To its glorious shining light?

How did the wise men know the Star
Would lead them to the King?
How did they choose the precious gifts
That each of them would bring . . .
The frankincense, the gold, the myrrh,
Gifts both costly and rare,
Presented to the Infant Child
As they knelt in homage there?

What if the Star of Bethlehem
Should shine this Christmas Eve?
Would we follow its rays to the stable small
And the Christ Child there receive?
Would we too kneel at His feet
And our gifts to Him present,
Or would we sleep, all unaware
Of the wonders of His advent?

O let us go to Bethlehem
And seek the Infant King,
Present to Him our gift of love—
What better could we bring?—
Kneel with the wise men from the East,
The shepherds on the hill,
And hear the heavenly host proclaim
To all, "Peace and good will."

©

What Can I Give Him?

Pamela Kennedy

The hauntingly beautiful carol "In the Bleak Midwinter" was composed as a Christmas poem in the late nineteenth century by an English woman born into a family gifted with artistic talent. Her verses vividly describe the birth of Christ as a personal encounter with the divine.

Christina Rossetti was the youngest of four children, born in 1830 to poet Gabriele Rossetti and his wife, Frances Polidori, a devout Anglican. All of Christina's siblings excelled in writing or painting, interpreting their Victorian world through the lens of art. From an early age she developed her talents, incorporating her father's flair for verse and her mother's religious piety.

At the age of eighteen, Christina, a sensitive and devout young woman, became engaged to James Collinson, a painter who was part of the Pre-Raphaelite Brotherhood, an art movement founded by her brother, Dante. When Collinson converted from Anglicanism to Catholicism, Christina broke their engagement and threw herself into her writing. Later that year, when her poetry was published in the *Athenaeum* magazine, she received critical praise, and some British critics suggested Rossetti as the natural successor to Elizabeth Barrett Browning as "female laureate." She produced a highly esteemed collection of poetry, though she never received Browning's degree of public acclaim.

When Christina's father was forced to retire due to blindness, financial troubles fell on the Rossetti family. Christina and her mother tried to establish a day school, though their venture did not succeed. After a second broken engagement, Christina devoted herself to social causes, all the while writing devotional pieces and poetry. She maintained a large circle of friends, including well-known artists and writers, such as Whistler, Swinburne, and Charles Dodgson (better known as Lewis Carroll, the author of *Alice's Adventures in Wonderland*).

It is not clear when she wrote "In the Bleak Midwinter," but it didn't become well known until ten years after her death, when her brother edited and published her complete works in 1904. It might never have been recognized as a great Christmas carol if Gustav Holst hadn't discovered it while helping to produce a new hymnal for the Anglican Church. He and composer Ralph Vaughan Williams sought beautiful poetry to set to original melodies suitable for congregational singing. Thus it was that Holst composed the hauntingly lovely tune for Rossetti's poem.

Set to Holst's music, Christina's words bring the Nativity to life through both divine and earthly images. The frozen earth "hard as iron, water like a stone" contrasts with the warmth of Mary's kiss and the worship of "angels and archangels." The final verse, inviting the singer to join shepherd and angel in worship of the infant Savior, has caused this carol to endure and remain a favorite for generations.

In the Bleak Midwinter

Christina Georgina Rossetti (1830–1894)　　　　　　　　　Gustav Holst (1874–1934)

Bits & Pieces

Great little One! whose all-embracing birth
Lifts Earth to Heaven, stoops Heaven to Earth.
—*Richard Crashaw*

The greatest Christmas gift of all
Was never placed beneath a tree
But lay within a manger bed,
Beneath a star, for all to see.
—*Emily Scarlett*

How can you make this the happiest Christmas of your life? Simply by trying to give yourself to others. Put something of yourself into everything you
give. A gift, however small, speaks its own language. And when it tells of
the love of the giver, it is truly blessed.
—*Norman Vincent Peale*

Remember, this December,
that love weighs more than gold!
—*Josephine Bacon*

Now Christmas comes, and the season culminates in the starlit hush of Christmas Eve and the glad events of Christmas Day. Now that the flurry of shopping, gift-wrapping, the decorating is over, let us enjoy and appreciate the sights and sounds, the joy and meaning of Christmas. Let us pause to remember that gift of love God sent to earth on that night so long ago, and to make room in our lives for Him whose birthday we now celebrate.
—*Esther York Burkholder*

Love came down at Christmas,
Love all lovely, love divine;
Love was born at Christmas.
—*Christina G. Rossetti*

There has been only one Christmas—the rest are anniversaries.
—*W. J. Cameron*

The light that shines from the humble manger is strong enough to lighten our way to the end of our days.
—*Author Unknown*

Nothing Shall Be Impossible

Luke 1:26–38

And in the sixth month the angel Gabriel was sent from God unto a city of Galilee, named Nazareth,

To a virgin espoused to a man whose name was Joseph, of the house of David; and the virgin's name was Mary.

And the angel came in unto her, and said, Hail, thou that art highly favoured, the Lord is with thee: blessed art thou among women.

And when she saw him, she was troubled at his saying, and cast in her mind what manner of salutation this should be.

And the angel said unto her, Fear not, Mary: for thou hast found favour with God. And, behold, thou shalt conceive in thy womb, and bring forth a son, and shalt call his name JESUS.

He shall be great, and shall be called the Son of the Highest: and the Lord God shall give unto him the throne of his father David: And he shall reign over the house of Jacob for ever; and of his kingdom there shall be no end.

Then said Mary unto the angel, How shall this be, seeing I know not a man?

And the angel answered and said unto her, The Holy Ghost shall come upon thee, and the power of the Highest shall overshadow thee: therefore also that holy thing which shall be born of thee shall be called the Son of God. And, behold, thy cousin Elisabeth, she hath also conceived a son in her old age: and this is the sixth month with her, who was called barren. For with God nothing shall be impossible.

And Mary said, Behold the handmaid of the Lord; be it unto me according to thy word. And the angel departed from her.

Painting by John Walter. Image from Ideals Publications

Unto the City of David
Luke 2:1–7

And it came to pass in those days, that there went out a decree from Caesar Augustus that all the world should be taxed. (And this taxing was first made when Cyrenius was governor of Syria.) And all went to be taxed, every one into his own city.

And Joseph also went up from Galilee, out of the city of Nazareth, into Judaea, unto the city of David, which is called Bethlehem; (because he was of the house and lineage of David:) To be taxed with Mary his espoused wife, being great with child.

And so it was, that, while they were there, the days were accomplished that she should be delivered.

And she brought forth her firstborn son, and wrapped him in swaddling clothes, and laid him in a manger; because there was no room for them in the inn.

Painting by John Walter. Image from Ideals Publications

Shepherds in the Field

Luke 2:8–20

And there were in the same country shepherds abiding in the field, keeping watch over their flock by night.

And, lo, the angel of the Lord came upon them, and the glory of the Lord shone round about them: and they were sore afraid.

And the angel said unto them, Fear not: for, behold, I bring you good tidings of great joy, which shall be to all people. For unto you is born this day in the city of David a Saviour, which is Christ the Lord.

And this shall be a sign unto you; Ye shall find the babe wrapped in swaddling clothes, lying in a manger.

And suddenly there was with the angel a multitude of the heavenly host praising God, and saying, Glory to God in the highest, and on earth peace, good will toward men.

And it came to pass, as the angels were gone away from them into heaven, the shepherds said one to another, Let us now go even unto Bethlehem, and see this thing which is come to pass, which the Lord hath made known unto us.

And they came with haste, and found Mary, and Joseph, and the babe lying in a manger.

And when they had seen it, they made known abroad the saying which was told them concerning this child. And all they that heard it wondered at those things which were told them by the shepherds.

But Mary kept all these things, and pondered them in her heart.

And the shepherds returned, glorifying and praising God for all the things that they had heard and seen, as it was told unto them.

Painting by John Walter. Image from Ideals Publications

Christmas Carol

Sara Teasdale

The kings they came from out the south,
All dressed in ermine fine;
They bore Him gold and chrysoprase,
And gifts of precious wine.

The shepherds came from out the north;
Their coats were brown and old;
They brought Him little newborn lambs—
They had not any gold.

The wise men came from out the east,
And they were wrapped in white;
The star that led them all the way
Did glorify the night.

The angels came from heaven high,
And they were clad with wings;
And lo, they brought a joyful song
The host of heaven sings.

The kings they knocked upon the door,
The wise men entered in,
The shepherds followed after them
To hear the song begin.

The angels sang through all the night
Until the rising sun,
But little Jesus fell asleep
Before the song was done.

Southport Methodist Church, Southport, Maine.
Photograph by William H. Johnson

Christmas in the Heart

Esther Lloyd Dauber

Have you sensed the charm of Christmas?
Have you seen the radiant star?
Heard the angels' alleluias
As they echo from afar?

Have you felt the pulse of church bells
In the magic, mystic air?
Grasped the tenor of excitement
That each being seems to share?

Have you glimpsed the sparkling radiance
In a child's bright eyes?
Have you awed in silent wonder
As you gazed at star-gemmed sky?

Have you marveled at the beauty
Of the caroler's sweet song?
Exchanged greetings, smiles, and laughter
As you walked amid the throng?

Have you thought about the manger
And the Babe that therein lay?
Has your heart swelled overflowing
With the love that came that day?

Then you have the Christmas spirit;
Never let its glow depart.
Peace and love will be your measure . . .
Always Christmas in your heart.

From CHRISTMAS IDEALS *1966*

Photograph by Dianne Dietrich Leis/Dietrich Photography

The Journey

Pamela Kennedy

I was ready to stop. We had traveled for months, and the initial excitement had long since worn off. Then shouts rang out: "There it is! The holy city! Jerusalem!" On the horizon, the city glistened in shades of cream and gold. We dismounted and set up camp at a small oasis.

As Magi, we spent our lives interpreting the relationship between the heavens and the earth. Combing through the ancient Hebrew Scriptures, we had discovered unusual prophecies in the Torah. The prophet Balaam predicted there would be a star coming out of the land of Jacob, heralding the birth of a king with divine powers—the long-awaited Messiah. When Jupiter emerged in the east as a morning star in Aries, the sign of the Jews, I knew it was the prophecy's fulfillment. Within weeks, we had begun our trek. Now we were in sight of our goal. Tomorrow we would reach our journey's end. I curled beneath my cloak on the still-warm earth and dreamed of thrones and crowns, of regal purple robes.

At first light, we made our way toward Jerusalem's gate. Old men sat discussing matters of the Law. Women bustled in the marketplace; roosters crowed and shopkeepers shouted, pointing to their wares. I approached a metalworker pounding out a copper pot.

"Where is the newborn king of the Jews?" I asked. "We have seen His star and have come to worship Him."

The fellow looked at me with guarded eyes. "There is no Lord but Caesar, and Herod is King of the Jews," he replied.

Around us a crowd gathered, murmuring. "Why have you come?" "Are you sent to trap us into treason?" "Leave us." "Herod is our king."

We moved on, and day after day we inquired, but no one would answer us. Then one morning a courier came. "His Majesty commands you to come." We were led to Herod's palace, where he received us in a richly decorated room. He scrutinized us with hard, dark eyes.

"I understand you have entered my city seeking a king," he began. I was reminded of a tiger—sleek, muscles poised to pounce. "I believe I can help you. I have had our priests and scholars search the Scriptures. Listen to what they discovered in the ancient writings of the prophet Micah." He unfurled a scroll and read: "'O Bethlehem of Judah, you are not just a lowly village in Judah, for a ruler will come from you who will be the shepherd for my people Israel.'"

My heart raced. The prophecy spoke of the One we sought!

Herod continued, "Go to Bethlehem and search for the child. And when you find Him, come back and tell me. It is my intent to also worship this newborn king." He smiled, but his eyes stayed cold. A shiver ran through me.

"As you wish, my lord." We bowed and left the chamber.

That evening we gathered our animals and headed to Bethlehem. It was dark; then suddenly the brilliant star reappeared! As we neared the town, it seemed to stand still, shedding its unearthly light on a single dwelling. We camped near an olive grove, waiting for morning.

When dawn slipped over the hilltops, I woke the others. Taking our small treasure casks, we wound through the narrow alleyways until we reached the house that that had been drenched in starlight. I knocked. A young woman opened the door and her eyes went wide as she took in our foreign attire.

"Please, we come to pay homage to the child," I explained quickly. "We bring gifts."

Then she smiled and beckoned us to enter. "Jesus," she said softly, and a little boy of just a year or so toddled out. "Please, sit," she offered and we settled upon low wooden benches.

The child grinned and clapped His hands, eyes dancing. We set our gifts on the floor and He plopped down, playing with the colorful chests.

We explained to Mary how we had come to find them, and she shared the story of His birth. We stared in wonder at the small child who bore so great a destiny. This was not the king I had expected. Yet, strangely compelled, I fell on my knees before Him in awe and adoration.

As we left, a voice whispered in my mind: "Do not return to Herod, for he plans to harm the child." Fear swept over me, and I turned for one last glance at the house. It stood in shadow now, the clouds covering the sun. Turning east, we departed on another road, picking up the pace as if chased by a sinister enemy. By nightfall we were miles away from Bethlehem . . . and Jerusalem. A new journey had begun.

I am an old man now, and there are many who believe my life is nearly over. But I know differently. For long ago in Bethlehem, I found much more than just an infant King. I discovered that knowing the Christ means one's journey never ends.

O Holy Night

Patsy Evans Pittman

*P*icture a perfect Christmas Eve, the air crisp and clear, the winter sky spattered with stars. My home is warm and festive on this holy night. Candles glow in the windows and encircle a treasured handmade créche that has been in our family since my children were babies. I don't know how long I will be able to resist the practicality of gas logs and an artificial tree, but for now a fire crackles in the fireplace and the scent of pine mingles with the lingering aroma of this evening's feast.

My guests have gone home, and I am alone, as I have been for the last six Christmases. I curl up on the couch to read the account of the birth of the Christ Child, and, because I am alone, I can read it aloud without feeling foolish. The majestic language of the King James Bible rolls from my tongue like poetry, almost too beautiful to bear.

I had not planned to attend the midnight service—Carols, Candles, and Communion—but a strange restlessness impels me from my warm nest into the crystal night. The streets are nearly deserted. Luminaries flicker in the median strip on Grand Central Avenue, stretching some thirty blocks to the outskirts of town. They also line the sidewalk in front of the church and both sides of the steps leading up to the sanctuary. Legend has it that these candles light the way of the Christ Child, but I think it's more likely they light our way to Him. I believe the Infant Jesus knew exactly where He was going. And why.

Scores of poinsettias decorate the chancel. The communion table is set. The lights are dimmed; the advent candles are in place. People—some in blue jeans and parkas and others in holiday finery—arrive by twos and threes and fours, quietly, awed by the miracle of this night. A soprano voice soars as the choir sings, "O, Holy Night!" Again, I hear the marvelous story of the virgin birth, this time from a newer version, recited from memory in the rich bass voice of our pastor.

Those of us assembled on this night sing carols to celebrate the holy birth; we take communion to commemorate His death. Then, as a final act of worship and thanksgiving, we pick up unlit candles and form a circle around the sanctuary. The lights are extinguished. Except for the Christ candle, the sanctuary is in darkness. A candle dips into that flame and passes to the next and the next and the next. A soft voice begins to sing "Silent Night," and, as the flame is passed, other voices join in. The sanctuary is bathed in the ever-widening circle of light, and the soft strains of the beloved carol, like a gentle wave, wash over the circle, around, and back again.

The last notes die away, the candles are snuffed out, and, silently, we file out into the night. It is exactly midnight, and as church bells peal out the glad tidings of Christmas morning, huge snowflakes drift down, softly, like a benediction.

Gold, Circumstance, and Mud

Rex Knowles

It was the week before Christmas. I was baby-sitting with our four older children while my wife took the baby for his checkup. (Baby-sitting to me means reading the paper while the kids mess up the house.)

Only that day I wasn't reading. I was fuming. On every page of the paper, as I flicked angrily through them, gifts glittered and reindeer pranced, and I was told that there were only six more days in which to rush out and buy what I couldn't afford and nobody needed. What, I asked myself indignantly, did the glitter and the rush have to do with the birth of Christ?

There was a knock on the door of the study where I had barricaded myself. Then Nancy's voice: "Daddy, we have a play to put on. Do you want to see it?"

I didn't. But I had fatherly responsibilities, so I followed her into the living room. Right away I knew it was a Christmas play, for at the foot of the piano stool was a lighted flashlight wrapped in swaddling clothes lying in a shoebox.

Rex, age six, came in wearing my bathrobe and carrying a mop handle. He sat on the stool, looked at the flashlight. Nancy, ten, draped a sheet over her head, stood behind Rex, and began, "I'm Mary and this boy is Joseph. Usually in this play Joseph stands up and Mary sits down. But Mary sitting down is taller than Joseph standing up, so we thought it looked better this way."

Enter Trudy, four, at a full run. She never has learned to walk. There were pillowcases over her arms. She spread them wide and said only, "I'm an angel."

Then came Anne, eight. I knew right away she represented a wise man. In the first place, she moved like she was riding a camel (she had on her mother's high heels). And she was bedecked with all the jewelry available. On a pillow she carried three items, undoubtedly gold, frankincense, and myrrh.

She undulated across the room, bowed to the flashlight, to Mary, to Joseph, to the angel, and to me and then announced, "I am all three wise men. I bring precious gifts: gold, circumstance, and mud."

That was all. The play was over. I didn't laugh. I prayed. How near the truth Anne was! We come at Christmas burdened down with gold—with the showy gift and the tinsely tree. Under the circumstances we can do no other; circumstances of our time and place and custom. And it seems a bit like mud when we think of it.

But I looked at the shining faces of my children, as their audience of one applauded them, and remembered that a Child showed us how these things can be transformed. I remembered that this Child came into a material world and in so doing eternally blessed the material. He accepted the circumstances, imperfect and frustrating, into which He was born, and thereby infused them with the divine. And as for mud—to you and me it may be something to sweep off the rug, but to all children it is something to build with.

Children see so surely through the tinsel and the habit and the earthly, to the love which, in them all, strains for expression.

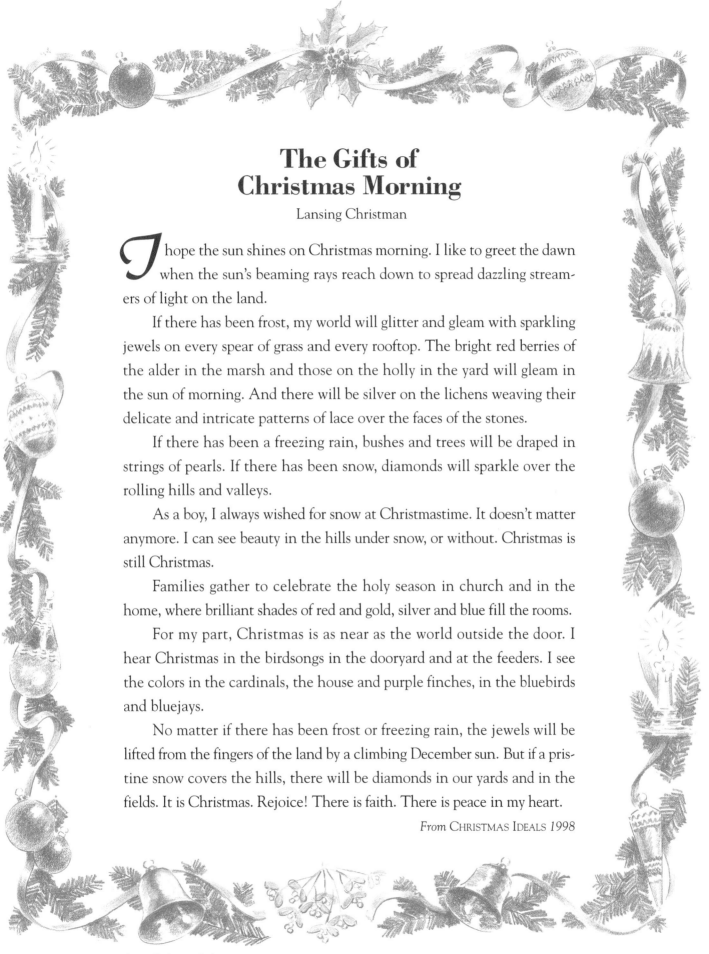

The Gifts of
Christmas Morning

Lansing Christman

I hope the sun shines on Christmas morning. I like to greet the dawn when the sun's beaming rays reach down to spread dazzling streamers of light on the land.

If there has been frost, my world will glitter and gleam with sparkling jewels on every spear of grass and every rooftop. The bright red berries of the alder in the marsh and those on the holly in the yard will gleam in the sun of morning. And there will be silver on the lichens weaving their delicate and intricate patterns of lace over the faces of the stones.

If there has been a freezing rain, bushes and trees will be draped in strings of pearls. If there has been snow, diamonds will sparkle over the rolling hills and valleys.

As a boy, I always wished for snow at Christmastime. It doesn't matter anymore. I can see beauty in the hills under snow, or without. Christmas is still Christmas.

Families gather to celebrate the holy season in church and in the home, where brilliant shades of red and gold, silver and blue fill the rooms.

For my part, Christmas is as near as the world outside the door. I hear Christmas in the birdsongs in the dooryard and at the feeders. I see the colors in the cardinals, the house and purple finches, in the bluebirds and bluejays.

No matter if there has been frost or freezing rain, the jewels will be lifted from the fingers of the land by a climbing December sun. But if a pristine snow covers the hills, there will be diamonds in our yards and in the fields. It is Christmas. Rejoice! There is faith. There is peace in my heart.

From CHRISTMAS IDEALS *1998*

Christmas Prayer

Elizabeth Searle Lamb

Dear God,
Let starshine light each heart.
Let peace line the humble crib.
Let love enfold this holy Child,
His story told by angel choir.
Oh, let all on earth together lift
Adoration for this, Thy greatest gift.
Amen.

From CHRISTMAS IDEALS *1980*

ISBN-13: 978-0-8249-1323-6

Published by Ideals Publications
A Guideposts Company
Nashville, Tennessee
www.idealsbooks.com

Publisher, Peggy Schaefer
Editor, Melinda Rathjen
Copy Editor, Michelle Prater Burke
Designer, Marisa Jackson
Permissions Editor, Patsy Jay

Cover: An *Old Fashioned Christmas* by Linda Nelson
Inside front cover: Painting by Ted Hoffmann. Image from Ideals Publications
Inside back cover: Painting by Ted Hoffmann. Image from Ideals Publications

Additional art credits:
"Bits & Pieces" art by Kathy Rusynyk; "In the Deep Midwinter" arranged and set by Dick Torrans;
A Christmas Morning by Lee Stroneck. Artwork courtesy of the artist and Wild Wings (www.wildwings.com)

ACKNOWLEDGMENTS:
KNOWLES, REX. "Gold, Circumstance, and Mud" from *Guideposts*, Dec. 1961, all rights reserved. NASH, OGDEN. "Old-Fashioned Cards" an excerpt from "Epstein, Spare That Yule Log," copyright © 1935. First published by Little, Brown. Used by permission of Curtis Brown, Ltd. PEALE, NORMAN VINCENT. "How can you make this the happiest Christmas . . ." a quote used by permission of The Peale Center. PORTER, ANNE, "When clustered sparks . . ." an excerpt from "Noël." Published in *Lving Things* by Zoland Books, an imprint of Steerforth Press. Copyright © 2006 by Anne Porter. Used by permission of the publisher. TABER, GLADYS. "Letter from Home," copyright © 1963 by author Gladys Taber. Reprinted by permission of Brandt and Hochman Literary Agents, Inc. TIPPETT, JAMES S. "Do Not Open Until Christmas" from *Counting the Days*. Copyright © 1940 by author James S. Tippett. Published by Harper & Bros. VAUGHN, BILL. "Tell Me a Story of Christmas" from *The Kansas City Star*. Used by permission, not an endorsement. All rights reserved. OUR THANKS to the following authors or their heirs: Deborah A. Bennett, Gail Brook Burket, Esther York Burkholder, Eleanor A. E. Chaffee, Lansing Christman, Gail O. Clark, Jeanne Conte, Esther Lloyd Dauber, Edgar A. Guest, Edna Jaques, Frank H. Keith, Pamela Kennedy, Elizabeth Searle Lamb, Judith Lane, Marcia Krugh Leaser, Alice Leedy Mason, Naomi I. Parks, Patsy Evans Pittman, Craig E. Sathoff, Nina Gertrude Smith, Eileen Spinelli, and Elisabeth Weaver Winstead.

Every effort has been made to establish ownership and use of each selection in this book. If contacted, the publisher will be pleased to rectify any inadvertent errors or omissions in subsequent editions.

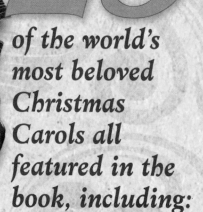